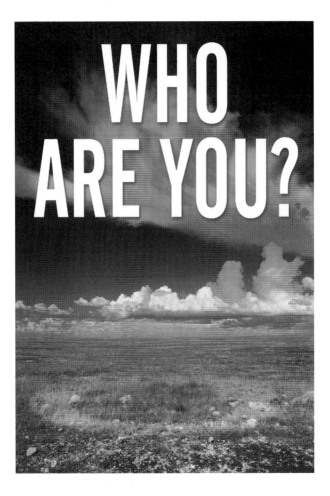

Also by Stedman Graham

You Can Make It Happen
You Can Make It Happen Every Day
Teens Can Make It Happen
Build Your Own Life Brand!
The Ultimate Guide to Sports Marketing
Move Without the Ball

Hay House Titles of Related Interest

Attitude Is Everything for Success, by Keith D. Harrell
Everything I've Ever Done That Worked,
by Lesley Garner
Five Steps for Overcoming Fear and Self-Doubt,
by Wyatt Webb
Passionate People Produce, by Charles Kovess
The Power of Intention, by Dr. Wayne W. Dyer
You Can Have an Amazing Life . . . in Just 60 Days!
by Dr. John F. Demartini

All of the above are available
at your local bookstore, or may be ordered by visiting:
Hay House USA: www.hayhouse.com
Hay House Australia: www.hayhouse.com.au
Hay House UK: www.hayhouse.co.uk
Hay House South Africa: orders@psdprom.co.za

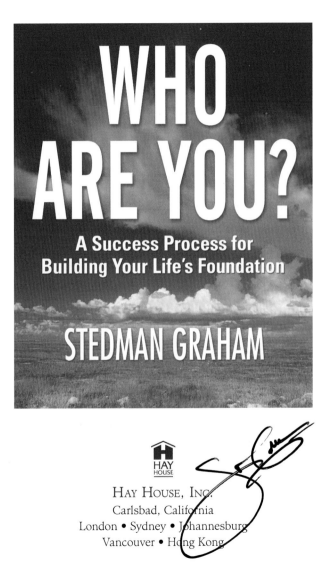

WHO ARE YOU?

A Success Process for Building Your Life's Foundation

STEDMAN GRAHAM

HAY HOUSE

HAY HOUSE, INC.
Carlsbad, California
London • Sydney • Johannesburg
Vancouver • Hong Kong

Published and distributed in the United States by: Hay House, Inc.,
P.O. Box 5100, Carlsbad, CA 92018-5100 • *Phone:* (760) 431-7695
or (800) 654-5126 • *Fax:* (760) 431-6948 or (800) 650-5115 • www.
hayhouse.com • *Published and distributed in Australia by:* Hay
House Australia Pty. Ltd., 18/36 Ralph St., Alexandria NSW 2015 •
Phone: 612-9669-4299 • *Fax:* 612-9669-4144 • www.hayhouse.com.
au • *Published and distributed in the United Kingdom by:* Hay House
UK, Ltd. • Unit 62, Canalot Studios • 222 Kensal Rd., London
W10 5BN • *Phone:* 44-20-8962-1230 • *Fax:* 44-20-8962-1239 • www.
hayhouse.co.uk • *Published and distributed in the Republic of South
Africa by:* Hay House SA (Pty), Ltd., P.O. Box 990, Witkoppen 2068
• *Phone/Fax:* 27-11-706-6612 • orders@psdprom.co.za • *Distributed
in Canada by:* Raincoast • 9050 Shaughnessy St., Vancouver, B.C.
V6P 6E5 • *Phone:* (604) 323-7100 • *Fax:* (604) 323-2600

Editorial supervision: Jill Kramer • *Design:* Amy Rose Szalkiewicz

Library of Congress Cataloging-in-Publication Data

Graham, Stedman.
  Who are you? : a success process for building your life's
foundation / Stedman Graham.
      p. cm.
  Includes bibliographical references.
  ISBN 1-4019-0346-0 (hardcover)
  1. Success--Psychological aspects. I. Title.
  BF637.S8G6835 2005
  158.1--dc22

                                          2004025568

              ISBN 13: 978-1-4019-0346-6
              ISBN 10: 1-4019-0346-0

              08 07 06 05   5 4 3 2
              1st printing, March 2005
              2nd printing, May 2005

        Printed in the United States of America

TO OPRAH,

a person who knows who she is, and who has helped me to know who I am. I marvel that you're the same whether you're talking to the President of the United States or to a homeless person on the street. You don't change. That's true authenticity, and that's the defining example of this book.

I REMEMBER HER AS A PERSON WHO GAVE ALL OF US A WORD OF ENCOURAGEMENT

I WANT to offer a special dedication to Mary Graham, my mother, who's 80 years young. She's a very special person, as all of us who know her would agree. I remember her as a person who gave all of us a word of encouragement—no matter who it was she was speaking to, she'd always give them a positive way to look at their situation. . . .

Mom, thank you for working the night shift for 25 years so that you could be home to make sure all six of us had clean clothes to wear and got to school on time. I can still hear you yell,"Steady, let's go, the bus is coming!" Thanks for taking the lead when Daddy got hurt and couldn't work. You, [my late brother] Irving, and I all had to pull together to take all kinds of work to keep things going. I remember how we'd sell fish door-to-door out of the back of the station wagon. I didn't quite understand the pressures you were under (at age 12 or 13, it was fun for me).

Mom, thanks for showing up at my basketball games; I'd always look for you in the stands. Thank you for involving me in so many activities and letting me go so many places. It's why I love to travel today.

Mom, most of all, thanks for giving me the spirit of never quitting or giving up, to see things through, regardless of the obstacles, and to have the empathy to be able to do what I do today. You've laid the foundation for understanding who I am. I think my father would be proud of both of us.

With love, your son,
Stedman

CONTENTS

WHEN WE LEARN TO PROCESS AND THINK, WE TAKE OWNERSHIP OF OUR LIVES

PREFACE

*"Each of us is in truth . . .
an unlimited idea of freedom."*

— Richard Bach

FREEDOM. This concept is defined as the capacity to exercise choice and autonomy, and the ability to enjoy life's privileges. In America, we talk about freedom and try to live it—but are we really free?

We live in a world where we buy in to the definitions of other people, allowing them to label us according to our race, gender, background, class, or environment. When we buy in to these labels, we put ourselves in boxes that limit us. The result is that we never realize our greatest potential.

From the moment we get up in the morning to the time we go to bed at night, most of our day is spent doing the same routine, seven days a week. Now, if we did the same thing yesterday that we're going to do today and tomorrow, what have we really done? The answer is: nothing. We're stuck in a comfort zone. Our days are filled with so many automatic activities that we never get a chance to think about why we're doing them and who we are.

The educational system is often of no help either. We sit in a classroom, read and study information, get tested, and are then labeled by a grade—but we don't always learn to *think*. Unfortunately, so many of us can relate to the process of learning and forgetting . . . so how is it possible to grow or develop when the information is never connected to our heart and soul, then to our mind, and finally to the world we live in? Consequently, the world ends up telling us: "You don't know who you are, so let me tell you."

This book doesn't attempt to solve all your problems or give you all the answers. However, it *is* designed to get you to think, and to jolt you out of that comfort zone. I hope that *Who Are You?* will help you start improving yourself every day by learning to process. You see, when we learn to process and think, we take ownership of our lives. Regardless of how someone else defines us, we're able to take control of knowing who we are, and that's a gift of freedom we give to ourselves.

WITH CHANGE
COMES
OPPORTUNITY
AND GROWTH

INTRODUCTION

"We must become the change we seek in the world."

— Mohandas Gandhi

EVERYWHERE you turn there are messages about success, as if there's one ultimate indicator or destination point that everyone who "makes it" reaches. In truth, there are probably millions of definitions of success: They range from tangibles such as a big salary, fancy house, expensive car, or corner office . . . to intangibles such as happiness, freedom, good health, and family. There are also some that are a little of both, such as education level, rank, or title.

Have you ever thought about what *your* definition of success is? It could very well be different from what it was ten years ago or even ten months ago, and it may change in the days to come, but please take a moment to really think about what it means to you.

Success and Self-Awareness

As you may have guessed, I've spent a lot of time considering my own definition of success. In fact, I've spent my entire life focusing on helping individuals and organizations become successful, no matter what their definition is. Through books, educational seminars, and consulting, my company, S. Graham and Associates (SGA), helps others arrive at their own definition through a step-by-step process based on their values and interests. We've worked with a wide range of people of all ages and economic levels to help them frame their lives for triumph. For me, success isn't just about financial or career achievement, it's about leading a *fully engaged life,* in which all your gifts and talents are developed and put to their highest use.

We've all heard that you can't know where you're going if you don't know where you've been. I'd add that if you don't know where you are today, you may drift into an unsatisfying, unsuccessful future. The unsatisfying part is key here: How many people do you know (perhaps including yourself) who feel as if they're in a job or relationship that may not be going anywhere? They're anxious or maybe even apathetic, feeling that they're not accomplishing anything for themselves or for others. This scenario is especially sad if they had

higher hopes and expectations for themselves at an earlier time.

There are also too many people who have met the expectations they originally set out to meet, but now feel empty and depressed. Maybe their "plan" consisted of making a certain salary or getting a particular title, but true happiness that comes from leading a meaningful and authentic life wasn't accounted for in that picture.

People want more out of life. They want to be fully engaged—they don't want to feel as if they're running in place and not progressing. No kid dreams of it, and no adult starts the day with that objective . . . it just happens. It's like seashells very gradually turning into sand from the pressure of the ocean and the wind: It occurs so slowly that you don't see it coming. In other words, you may want to go down a certain path, but you take a little detour . . . and then another . . . and before you know it, you don't know how to move forward—or even how to go back to where you started.

It's not too late to get back on track (or to start on the right one). That's the good news. There is no bad news, except that it will take a little— okay, a lot—of soul-searching. But the other good news is that this is a journey you'll enjoy because it's all about you and what you enjoy doing. To that end, parents are sometimes surprised to see their teenagers, who never liked to read, finish my books *Teens Can Make It Happen* or *Move Without the Ball* cover to cover—even foregoing the usual TV, phone, or video-game time. Now these books aren't filled with the latest gossip about the kids' favorite sports or movie stars, nor are they about anything illicit that may be appealing to rebellious teens. They're not even light reading! Yet teens are just like adults: They're interested in a subject if that subject is themselves, and that's what those books are about.

Gaining self-awareness—and then doing something about it—isn't a task that everyone's willing to take on. Many people are content with things the way they are, while others may desire greater success but don't want to put out the effort to improve themselves. One possible reason is they don't even realize that they have the power to do something about their lives.

In other words, if you don't have the awareness that there is a problem, or if you don't think that you have the ability to change your circumstances, you're going to stay right where you are.

A big stumbling block that I see among people of all ages when I talk to them about knowing who they are is *fear*. Fear is a very powerful motivator to do or not to do something. People may dread exploring their past or examining their weaknesses, or they may not want to be reminded of painful experiences or made to feel that they lack value. Many people are also afraid of success itself and how that might change their lives. They get so comfortable with the status quo that any uncertainty—good or bad—can seem threatening. There are many who sabotage their own success because they don't feel that they deserve it.

Fear of self-knowledge is common and natural. Motivational psychologist Abraham Maslow, father of the theory of self-actualization, said that we fear the truth at the same time we seek it: "For instance, certain truths carry automatic responsibilities, which may be anxiety-producing," he explained. "One way to evade the responsibility and the anxiety is simply to evade consciousness of the truth."

The good news is that through the act of looking inward to seek your true self, you'll be taking responsibility *and* moving toward self-actualization.

The Success Process

Right now I'd like you to take a moment to discover what your ultimate aim in reading this book is. Ask yourself, "What will I do in my life to feel successful? What will I stand for that others will admire about me?"

You're probably beginning to realize that we have to work as a team here: I can provide the questions or elicit some from you, but you're the one who must provide the answers. What I can also offer you is a process to align yourself with the resources to make your vision of success a reality. You're responsible for *planning to succeed,* which takes place naturally as you commit to this process every day.

The "Nine Steps to Success" curriculum that I share with people is a systematic approach to organizing and advancing life goals and aspirations. It's the *how:* It enhances your focus, organization, and time-management skills; helps improve relationships; enables you to change how you think about yourself and your possibilities; and encourages you to recognize and analyze attitudes and behaviors that stand in the way of success. It shows you how to appreciate and invest in yourself, for example, by valuing educational, health, and career-preparation opportunities, which are keys

to achieving individual excellence; and it provides tools for managing stress and emphasizing the long-term consequences of individual behavior.

Here's a brief summary of the Nine Steps, along with some questions and suggestions to help you work through each one:

Step 1: Check Your ID

Before you decide what you want out of your life, you must first understand who you are, what the influences on your life are, and why you think and act the way you do. Self-awareness is where success begins—it's difficult to understand the world and how you respond to it until you first know yourself.

What are your strengths (that is, what moves you forward)? What are your weaknesses (what holds you back)? What are your patterns of behavior? What are your passions? Sometimes the biggest obstacles to success are those that you unconsciously put in your own path—such as past hurts, business or career downfalls, and negative attitudes—and they hold you back. Learn from the bad experiences and failures, and let them go.

Step 2: Create Your Vision

Realizing and exploring your dreams and aspirations should be your life's destination. Having a vision will help you on your journey because it will keep you focused and minimize distractions. A well-defined vision enables you to set meaningful goals for your business or personal life, while a lack of one will severely weaken your leadership skills.

How do you envision your future? Describe the short- and long-term wishes you have for your life personally and professionally.

Step 3: Develop Your Travel Plan

If you're going to fulfill your vision for a better life, you must create a plan of action. When you begin to work toward your goals by doing so, you assert power over your life. You know who you are, where you're going, and how you're going to get there. Planning saves time, keeps you focused, and builds confidence.

Your personal travel plan should consider family, community, and friends, as well as client relationships, your co-workers/employees/boss, and business growth.

Step 4: Master the Rules of the Road

You need guidelines to keep you on track as you pursue a better life. The rules are constant and enduring; they do not change. Characteristics to guide your life are:

- honesty,
- hard work,
- determination, and
- a positive attitude.

Step 5: Step In to the Outer Limits

In order to grow, you must first leave your comfort zone by confronting your fears and taking risks. Fear of the unknown is one of the greatest obstacles that you'll face when taking this journey. Keep in mind that if you're going to be successful, you must learn to overcome that natural fear and step outside what's become comfortable and familiar. Key points to remember:

- Risk is a natural part of life.
- Staying the same is standing still.
- Change (growth) means risk.

Step 6: Pilot the Seasons of Change

If you keep doing what you've always done, you'll get the same results—so learn how to create change and manage your response to it. Dealing with changing circumstances is important, but creating and managing your *response* to change is probably an even greater part of the Nine Steps to Success. Challenges happen when the pace of change exceeds our ability to catch up, and events move faster than our understanding. But remember: With change comes opportunity and growth.

Step 7: Build Your Dream Team

No one makes it alone, so learn to trust and be trustworthy. Build supportive relationships that will help you work toward your goals—you're going to need the encouragement of others.

With a great team assisting you, you can do more than you could ever do alone. Surround yourself with people who *care* about you and believe in your goals. Trust is critical to building a strong support team. And note that credibility comes with a pattern of behavior: Trust isn't easily earned—it's established over time.

Step 8: Win by a Decision

What you are in this world is largely the result of the decisions you've made so far. The choices that you make on your path from hereon in will be some of your greatest challenges.

How can you tell the difference between a good and a bad decision? Good decisions have desirable consequences (they help you grow and reach your goals), while bad decisions have undesirable consequences. Continue to maximize your decision-making ability by considering the personal as well as professional impact of your choices.

Step 9: Commit to Your Vision

Devote your time and energy on a consistent basis to pursuing your goals. Enthusiasm and commitment generate excellence, and that leads to success. A commitment is something you live—and renew and fulfill—every day. It's *doing* rather than *saying.*

WHO ARE YOU?

As You Begin . . .

Below I've summarized some of the key points I want to emphasize as you work through this book:

- To know yourself is the first and most important step in the Success Process.

- Self-understanding is a lifelong pursuit.

- Once you have a sense of who you are, you can then begin to envision who you want to become.

- You can control your life by controlling the way you think.

- It's vital that you replace negative messages with more positive ones.

- Consider your personality, talents, and gifts so that you can give your all to everything you do.

- Move toward positions that naturally fit your strengths and passions.

- Work to connect with people you like and respect and who, in turn, like and respect you.

- Believe in the *possibilities* for your life.

Once you know how to fire up your engine (as well as what fuels it), you can then determine a direction for your life. However, keep in mind that you won't go anywhere without the first step: "Who are you?"

So my challenge to you is to become personally accountable for your success by making education and information relevant to your world. In these pages, I'll show you how to access resources and think differently about them—and consequently, you'll begin to think differently about yourself. You'll see yourself as the star you are. Everybody wants to be a winner—the difference is in knowing *how*.

Ladies and gentlemen, start your engines.

CHAPTER ONE

THE WORLD WE LIVE IN

"Things do not happen;
things are made to happen."

— John F. Kennedy

THE WORLD is a collection of unlimited wealth and resources—yet we often limit our potential by moving in our own small circles because of our fears. If we change the way we view the world, there's nothing we can't accomplish.

I think that the greatest opportunity in life is to have a sense of who you are. To me, that means being comfortable with yourself and your surroundings. It's connecting to what's real and being able to feel your authenticity. It's looking past labels. It's having clarity about your life and your possibilities by viewing your life from a higher point than where you are now. It's being able to establish a personal- and professional-performance program to

1

build, leverage, and position yourself in your chosen area of influence. It's wanting to perform up to your potential—and being able to do so.

Your success is based on your *commitment to discovery:* first, discovering who you are; second, discovering how to apply this knowledge to the world you live in; and third, making the discovery process part of your daily routine to sustain success over a lifetime. The challenge lies in the ability to coexist and grow with the world as it changes, rather than collide with it or get swallowed up in it.

It took me a long time to understand that the world we live in is defined by and programmed by so many external things—including our family, school, job, and friends . . . not to mention the messages we get from the media. With so many agendas coming at me all the time, I often have to step back and ask myself, "At this time, what's my program? What messages am I listening to about what I should do, what I should want, where I should live, and what kind of car I should drive?" After all, the messages I've been listening to and following might be very different from what I really need and want.

I know of no greater feeling than having clarity of purpose in life so that I can focus my energy

and resources on my goals and visions. Taking a proactive approach to creating opportunities rather than waiting for things to happen has helped save me many years of wasted time. And it's had a positive domino effect: I'm rewarded at many levels when I have clarity because I can more easily align the resources available to me for continued progress. This progress builds momentum and creates more opportunities.

During my journey through life, I've learned that there are many important things that people have in common, no matter what city, state, country, or continent they're from. People want leadership—they want to follow a model, or someone who knows where to go and how to get there. In a world often clouded by uncertainty and fear, the ability to articulate a clear vision and plan is as desirable as principle-guided leadership, although the two need not be mutually exclusive. They also want to be valued—they want their achievements recognized, and they want to feel good about themselves. And folks also want to be better—they want to know how they can build even more value for themselves in the future. In addition, I've learned that not much is accomplished when you focus on others' shortcomings. I've found it more valuable to focus on opportunities rather than on problems and weaknesses.

3

The Routine of Life

Most of us live in a routine—that is, there's a predictable pattern to what we do every day. When I speak to groups, I often ask them what their daily routines are. Not to my surprise, they tell me basically the same thing no matter where I'm speaking: Early in the morning most people get up, shower, brush their teeth, maybe grab a quick breakfast, and get the kids off to school; then they drive or take a train or bus to work, spend eight or more hours at the job doing the same types of things every day; and then they get the kids, go home, eat dinner, watch TV, and go to bed. This is pretty much a template for the entire workweek. On Friday nights, maybe folks go out; while on Saturday they try to sleep in a little and then do chores such as grocery shopping or mowing the lawn. (They may go out again on Saturday night.) On Sunday, they might go to church, have dinner with the family, and then get ready for Monday. How long can this routine be kept up? Some of us might say for 30 years, or even all our lives.

Well, when we look back after 30 years, we'll find that we have no more in the end than we had in the beginning. That's because we can't keep doing the same thing and expecting different results. We stunt our personal and professional

growth if we don't strive to do and be something better tomorrow than yesterday and today.

Most of our time *is* spent doing mundane tasks: sleeping, eating, driving, dressing, bathing and grooming, checking and replying to e-mails, paying bills, watching TV, trying to organize paperwork, and making sure the kids get to the bus on time. Even celebrities, who we imagine lead glamorous and exciting lives 24/7, have a lot of normalcy in their routine. Humans across cultures—and across the globe—play out these same scenarios every day.

There's nothing wrong with the concept of a routine. What I'm saying is that when we're focusing on them, they should be *thoughtfully based on what we want to accomplish.* As philosopher Henry David Thoreau put it: "It is not enough to be industrious; so are the ants. What are you industrious about?" Good routines aren't automatic, because in doing them we're more aware of *what* we're doing and *why.* More than that, the key to making routines work for us is to improve upon them every day.

Care

The word *care* is very important in our lives because without it, we disconnect. We're just going through the motions. Whenever I read the newspaper, or travel and speak to people, I realize that lack of care is a huge problem in our society—we just aren't doing a very good job of tending to ourselves or anyone else. (Think about it: Isn't that the source of all types of problems today?) And we first have to learn to care for ourselves before we can care for others.

As individuals, we may not eat right, get enough sleep or exercise, or reach out for the support or affection we need. If we do take this type of care— that is, we look out for and show some concern and tenderness toward ourselves—we'll be way ahead in life and weather its rough storms.

Lack of care can become a dark, spiraling path that leads to serious family and societal problems. For example, if you're apathetic about your job, it will show in your work. People say that things used to be made with more care, and in many cases that's true—in our fast-paced, bottom-line-focused world, we often sacrifice quality. There may also be multiple people involved at different stages of a project or product's development so that no one individual feels the responsibility or pride he would have felt if he had control, or had at least contributed to the big picture. There's a loss of ownership of the end product or service as well. Likewise, if you're a teacher and you don't like your

job, think about the effect that could have on the students in your classroom. And if you don't care about your neighbors or community as a whole, they're going to suffer. You ultimately do, too.

This reminds me of when I was on a ten-city tour for *Teens Can Make It Happen*. I spoke with corporate and community leaders and also visited schools at each stop. As I got out of the car at one particular school in Denver, I saw trash all over the schoolyard. A tennis court for the students was terribly run-down: The surface was all cracked and covered with debris, weeds, and overgrown bushes. Then as I walked up to the school itself, I noticed that the building was dingy and badly in need of a paint job, and a couple of the windows were cracked. It was actually a great-looking structure—the architecture was fabulous—but it needed a lot of work. I wondered how in the world the students could care about themselves or their education when they were walking into this environment every single day. How could they be expected to care when the people running the school didn't seem to?

I immediately went into "vision mode." I asked myself, "What would it take to make this environment better? I know that the public-education system doesn't have a lot of money to work with, but how much does it cost to pick up the garbage around the school or cut the grass? It wouldn't take that much to get the building painted—they could even raise a collection to do it. Obviously, nobody cares."

And that's precisely the message that these kids got every single day when they took the walk toward their classrooms. When I spoke to the students, my intuition was confirmed: They were lifeless—the neglect and lack of concern was evident in their hollow expressions.

We each have a daily decision to make about how we tend to ourselves and others in our community. When we put out the effort—even a small one—to care, we start to feel good about our community, our relationships, and ourselves.

"How do I do this?" you may ask. Well, good intentions for caring are a great start, but in order to *ensure* and *sustain* care, accountability has to be part of the equation. You want to hold yourself accountable and allow people you trust to hold you accountable, too. It often takes someone who knows you well but isn't close to your current situation to bring to your attention your lack of care, be it in yourself, your work or studies, or your relationship. A good friend, relative, mentor, or supervisor will make you accountable for your actions or inaction because she truly does care about you and feels that she knows what's best for you.

The beautiful thing that happens when others believe in you is this: During those times when you've

given up on yourself, they haven't. If your friend cares about you, he's invested in your success—therefore, he'll refuse to see you compromise your future happiness in a moment of temporary doubt. Just think how many more teens could be convinced to stay in school, stay clean, or apply for college if they had an honest rapport with someone who cared.

The Power of Relevancy

One of the reasons our school systems aren't up to par is because they tend to miss the connection between young people and their personal development. It doesn't make sense, but the educational system—which can be the greatest influence on our lives for positive change, no matter what our circumstances are—is one of the many institutions that actually discourages us from thinking.

Much of what I believe is wrong with the state of education today in America, where more money is spent per pupil than in almost any other nation, is that it's driven by the labels of grades. When grades or scores are of primary importance (versus relevant learning), the natural result is that teachers begin to "teach to tests"—consequently, students memorize, spit back the information on an exam or essay, and then quickly forget it. The culture of cheating that's been sweeping across our country—at all social and economic levels—is just a symptom of this type of education. What's important to the students isn't necessarily of any importance to the teachers or school, so the students quickly learn that their thoughts or opinions don't carry much weight. In other words, why try to think?

The same goes for the work environment: People who talk about changing the status quo aren't admired or promoted—on the contrary, they're seen as threatening or wanting to create more work and problems. Instead, employees are encouraged to punch in, do what they're told, break for lunch, and come back and do the same thing for four or five more hours. No thinking required. And when free thinking is discouraged, *freedom* is discouraged.

In order to get in touch with who you really are—and subsequently be the best you can be—you need to think in terms of how the information and resources you have access to can directly propel your success. Not everything will be relevant, but some of it will be. If you want to rise above mediocrity and create a successful, satisfying life, you need to be proactive in seeking information and resources, and not wait for it to come to you as it does in school.

To get a feel for what I'm talking about, flip through a newspaper or magazine today and make a conscious effort to pull out three things—information, advice,

or ideas—that you might be able to benefit from in your personal or professional life. Here's an example: In the financial section, you learn about a retail company that's making unusual gains in the market. Do you want to research more about the company to see if you might want to apply for a job or consider purchasing stock or a franchise? If you have your own business, what tips would you like to evaluate and possibly use yourself? What's their management structure like? What's made their marketing campaign successful? Does the company sell a product or service that fills a need you have?

If you're involved with a charity or community organization, could you solicit this company to sponsor or host a future event? Might they donate products for an auction or directly to your program beneficiaries? Maybe they'd be willing to support your local school by purchasing ad space or offering coupons in a publication. You see, when you start to think about making information relevant to your life and the lives of those around you, you can see how it can lead to endless opportunities.

Build on Your Strengths

By committing to thinking and self-learning, you'll have a way to continue to absorb knowledge and make it relevant to your life. You know that you aren't as likely to pursue learning—and you're a lot less likely to retain information—if it isn't relevant to your life. There are trivia buffs and news junkies among us (myself included) who retain lots of seemingly useless knowledge, but in reality it relates to an interest or need we have. Once we're aware of our interests and needs, we'll naturally gravitate toward activities and information that satisfy them.

Likewise, students of all ages tend to pay the most attention to subjects that are of interest to them and that they see themselves making achievements in. If you feel you have some affinity for playing the piano, for instance, then you're more likely to want to continue to take lessons. However, if you're convinced that you have no musical aptitude whatsoever, then you'll probably think that it would be a waste of time to pursue this avenue.

For younger students who are still exploring different fields, such as developing their reading and writing skills, competence should be attained in all areas. Then as they enter high school, those who are excelling in a particular area such as math should continue and strive for excellence. Although intelligent people often perform well in multiple areas, this doesn't tend to hold true across the board—someone might be brilliant in science but horrible at English, for example. You could probably list your

strengths and weaknesses back in elementary and high school, no matter how long ago you attended. This is something we all recall because we remember how good success felt and how terrible failure felt.

In my seminars, I teach students that failure is necessary for growth, and all people who are successful fail sometimes—that's how we often learn best. By the same token, if you've ever participated in a spelling bee, I'll bet that you'll always remember how to spell the word that disqualified you. That's a very simple example of how we can learn from our failures, but there are many more complex ways. If you ever tried to start your own business, then you know that there are always hardships—so many things you didn't predict, couldn't control, or could have done better. It's easy to lose perspective and think that the world will end because you made a bad decision, didn't get accepted to a certain school, or missed out on a certain job. The solution is always the same: You must face your fear of failure in order to move ahead.

How can you develop the courage to keep going despite discouragements and distractions? To start, you must believe in yourself and in your unique abilities—and that brings us to our next chapter.

LET
EXCELLENCE
BE THE BRAND
THAT PEOPLE
ASSOCIATE
WITH YOU

CHAPTER TWO

BELIEVE IN YOURSELF

"It's lack of faith that makes people afraid of meeting challenges, and I believed in myself."
— Muhammad Ali

WE CAN NEVER hope to know all the answers to life, so many of us have faith in a higher power or that some things are "meant to be." Believing in something outside of yourself is a personal decision. It can help you find peace and meaning in life; and it can motivate you to act compassionately, honestly, and with courage. My cautionary advice, however, is to forego surrendering all your control and purpose to an outside force. It can be a crutch, a way to write off failure by saying, "Well, I guess it just wasn't meant to be," instead of thinking about how you can try again and do things differently the next time.

So as you seek life's answers, I encourage you to look for information not only from the spiritual realm, but also from within your circle of acquaintances. Friends, co-workers, and family members whom you feel comfortable around and with whom you can "be yourself" can often give you some good and honest insight. (One caveat: You can't get too upset with them if you ask for honesty and they tell you something you don't want to hear!)

Insight is the perfect word to describe what I'm talking about here. To know yourself, you must learn to look *inward*—only then can you contribute your gifts to others in the fullest and most meaningful way. We all have gifts; some of us just haven't unwrapped them yet. Yours are as different from everyone else's as your DNA is: You may think that you know what they are, and you could be right, but often that isn't the case. As management expert Peter F. Drucker says, "Most people think they know what they are good at. They are usually wrong. People know what they are *not* good at more often—and even there people are more often wrong than right. And yet, a person can perform only from strength."

The Most Powerful Word in the World

The most powerful word in the world is spelled *l-o-v-e*. Loving yourself is really the key to success—and you have to learn to do this, in spite of pressures to do otherwise. Unfortunately, many businesses make their money by trying to keep you dissatisfied with yourself. For example, there are countless makeover TV shows and magazines, along with an entire field of image consultants who offer tips (at a steep price) for wardrobe management, as well as recommendations for changing your body, voice, or body language. You can reduce, refine, or augment through plastic surgery, liposuction, and gastric-bypass surgery; be the envy of the neighbors with a new car, boat, or motorcycle; and stock up on herbs, pharmaceuticals, spa treatments, energy drinks, tooth whiteners, or whatever panacea is currently the rage.

Advertising works because it targets our deep fears and desires about how others perceive us. It also works because these products and procedures only *temporarily* make us feel better about ourselves. That way, we can keep buying again and again. But what these companies really sell are illusions—and we've got to fight against all those programs that try to mold our external package.

This external focus especially affects young people. While problems such as childhood and teen obesity are widespread, so are body-image problems for both sexes. We're moving away from just being *self*-conscious to now being *publicly* conscious about our appearance. Popular discussion threads in online communities for teens are "Rate Me/Rate My" activities, where young people post photos of different parts of their body and ask other members to rate them on a scale of 1 to 10. This probably stems from the popularity of TV and radio shows that critique the physique of approval-seeking guests, who either tend to have very low self-esteem or an overabundance of it. The teens doing the posting probably represent the same ends of this spectrum, and they hope that the public's acceptance will make them feel better about themselves or validate their vanity.

But what's at *your* core? You're not an empty, flesh-covered mannequin—although you might feel that way without self-knowledge. You have life energy; and you have beliefs, values, passions, relationships, principles, and fears. Of course these important aspects can't be seen as easily as your hair or skin color, or whether you're tall or short, thin or fat. That's just the "packaging" around who you are.

It concerns me that so much time, energy, and money is focused on that outer shell. I won't go so far as to say this shell doesn't matter—because it does influence how others perceive us and how we perceive ourselves. But that's only because we allow ourselves to give value—very high value—to this veneer. However, *we* can decide what we're going to base our self-worth upon.

Illuminating Life's Illusions

All the pop-culture messages I've talked about here give people the illusion that love—including self-love—can be bought. In reality, individuals who really do love themselves aren't so influenced by material things. For example, they're not spending much energy or money trying to live up to others' fashion rules—they're often the trendsetters themselves.

This self-acceptance also shows up in how these people deal with day-to-day frustrations. As they weather a job loss, breakup, or house fire, for example, they remain grateful and positive—even as those around them feel despair and consequently self-destruct. You can sense that they're happy from the inside out: They're not looking for approval from others, because they've filled the hole in their hearts with self-acceptance.

When you fill the hole in your own heart, you become a whole person. You're at peace with yourself and with the world. That doesn't mean that you'll feel superior to, or more beautiful than, other people or that your hardships will go away. You'll still confront the same challenges, but with more courage, focus, and determination. Painful experiences will still be painful, but you'll create more experiences of joy to balance them out—and tip the scale to the positive.

Now you may be wondering, *How do I learn to fill the hole in my heart and love myself?* Well, first you need to find out *what you love to do.* This will lead you to self-love. As you pursue your passions, you'll feel happy and engaged in life. You'll naturally take joy and pride in the activities you do well, and you'll notice that regardless of other circumstances, you have something positive to focus on. When you're able to direct your attention toward something you love, it grows—just like a gardener tending to a favorite rosebush, or a parent cuddling a small child.

If you focus your attention on your problems, they'll grow, too . . . so don't spend your time on activities that you don't enjoy or that don't get you anywhere. I know it's easier said than done: You

have to pay the bills, and your job may help you do that—even if you dread going to work every morning. If that's the case, set your sights on something you'll look forward to doing each day, and take mini-steps toward that new career path.

This past Christmas I received a lovely portrait as a gift. I had the good fortune to meet the artist, Sharon Lynn Campbell, in person and learn her story. People who choose a career in the creative arts go against the grain of our society—which values practical jobs that earn a decent wage—so I'm always interested in hearing how they "make it work."

Sharon spent her days painting faux finishes in people's homes to make a living, knowing all along that what she wanted to do was classic portraiture. She gave her best effort and earned the respect of her clients, but after a full day's work, this mom of three pushed herself to paint every evening. She recognized the need to develop a portfolio of her fine art if she wanted to prosper through her passion. When she built up enough samples—and self-confidence—she slowly began mentioning to her faux-finish clientele that she was also a portrait artist. Through these clients, she received some commissions for portraiture, and soon word of her talent spread.

Instead of working as a faux-finish painter for 100 percent of her income, Sharon reduced that to

90 percent and spent the remainder with her oils, canvases, and subjects. Then the ratio changed to 70/30, then 50/50, and so on. It wasn't easy and it wasn't overnight success, but keeping her dream in mind kept her going through the rough times. Now she exclusively supports herself and her family as a successful classic-portrait artist. *Slow but steady progress toward a goal is the best method for attaining and sustaining success.*

Ask yourself the following: "If money wasn't an issue, what would I volunteer my time to do just for fun? What types of responsibilities would I have? What skills would I be using?" Now make a list of all the things you love—right here in this book. There are no right or wrong answers, and nothing's too big or too small to mention. Just list them as they come to mind:

_____	_____
_____	_____
_____	_____
_____	_____
_____	_____
_____	_____

—————————————   —————————————

—————————————   —————————————

—————————————   —————————————

Focusing on something positive really does make positive things happen (Buddhists and Hindus call it "creating good karma"). If you're not sure exactly what you love to do, consider helping out a cause you believe in by offering whatever talents or experience you have. Be willing to try new things, too—you might discover other interests and develop new talents along the way. Even if you don't, focusing on something that makes you feel as if you're contributing to a greater good is invaluable to yourself and to those you'll be helping.

In the Zone

People talk about being "in the zone," or doing something that comes so naturally to them and engages them to such a degree that time simply flies by. They may even say that they "lose themselves" in an activity or task. As I mentioned, human-motivation psychologist Abraham Maslow wrote about self-actualization, the highest state of our functioning, where more "earthly" needs and desires become less important, similar to Buddhahood. Self-actualization is the achievement of one's full potential through creativity, independence, spontaneity, and a grasp of the real world.

When you're doing something you love and challenging yourself to grow at the same time, you can experience this wonderful focus and feeling. Can you recall a time when you lost yourself in an activity and felt that all your talents were stretched to their limits? Being in the zone energizes and exhilarates, even though the work may be exhausting. You feel at one with the project, optimistic and strong.

Being in the zone can happen naturally, but you can also encourage it by stimulating the right hemisphere of your brain, your creative nature. You can doodle, hum, visualize, or try writing with your nondominant hand. Allow yourself the freedom to ask the "What if?" and "Why not?" questions. Practice being nonjudgmental when listening to or reading about new approaches. You can challenge yourself to do one of your daily routines in a different way or set and try to break time limits for these activities (for example, filing papers or folding laundry). If you tend to make presentations by reading directly from reports or

slide presentations, practice speaking off-the-cuff or from an outline.

One important thing to mention about being in the zone is to challenge but not overwhelm yourself. There's a happy medium for every activity, and *only you* can determine what that is. You know how much work you need to do during a day so that it goes by quickly and you're not bored and restless. You also know how much is too much—when you feel your muscles tightening and your tone of voice getting shorter, or you find yourself looking for ways to procrastinate.

Labels

How many African Americans in this country believe that they can't make it because of the color of their skin? How many women are discouraged from certain careers? Even if you're white, you can't escape labels from your family or from your environment.

We generally don't realize that we buy in to these labels, but whenever we take one on, it limits our identity in our own (and others') eyes. People like such identifiers because they're the easiest way to quickly put others in a box so that they'll know how to address them, how much time and energy to spend building a relationship with them, and how to use them in the future. Somewhere in there is a genuine interest in getting to know these new people, but it's usually only *after* a first meeting that the decision is made to keep relating to them. It may be based on their looks, profession, or family; whom they know; or upon learning that they share your interests.

Does this sound cold and shallow? Are you saying, "That's not me; that's not what I do"? I'm not trying to make anyone feel bad by this discussion; I just want to point out the natural tendencies we all have in our social interactions.

Branding

Much of labeling is actually based on time. Time is our most precious resource because it allows us the gift of life experience—because it's so valuable to us, we're always consciously (and unconsciously) looking for ways to save it. So if we can sum up a person's value in a few moments, that saves us a lot of time determining how to interact with the individual. We can't follow him around for days on end, interview his friends and neighbors, go to his workplace to see what he does

and the paychecks he receives, quiz him on facts that are important to us, or see how he treats loved ones and enemies—nor do we really want to. So labels suffice for our needs.

Now some people won't want to get to know us right off the bat based upon how we look. We may be a different race, we may be wearing odd clothing, we might not be in the same age range, we could have lots of piercings and tattoos, we may be in a wheelchair, or perhaps we were heard speaking to someone in a language other than English. This may not be fair or just, but it's often true.

The same can apply the other way: For example, young people who are trying to define themselves as individuals may intentionally dress and talk differently from what's accepted and expected in mainstream society. It's so common and widespread that there's even a name for it: teenage rebellion. Sometimes separating themselves for a while from what everybody does can be helpful in creating teens' own authentic identity. It may be different from how their parents want to see them, or even what their friends expect of them—but it's a natural part of the process of self-discovery. Once they find what "fits" and are comfortable in their own skin, they have less to prove or explore; rebelling for rebellion's sake subsides.

In other words, you're going to be stuck with some labels, while others you'll have more control over—but you have the ability to transcend them *all* by making education and life experiences relevant to your heart, soul, and mind. And then you'll need to apply this to the American free-enterprise system, which is the world we live in every single day. In other words, you can give yourself labels of your own creation, based on your own true self and how you want to be perceived in the world. This is what I call "branding."

In my book *Build Your Own Life Brand,* I encourage readers to use the time-tested strategies of marketing professionals for their own success. In advertising terms, branding is the "image" that's created in the minds of people when they see or hear a particular name, product, or logo. Over time, strong brands inspire trust by constantly keeping their promise of quality.

Let excellence be the brand that people associate with you. When you take the focus off your labels and put it on excellence, you'll empower yourself. Oprah Winfrey (my partner) and I share a strong belief that she articulates eloquently: "I was raised to

believe that excellence is the best deterrent to racism or sexism. And that's how I operate my life."

Each and every day, you demonstrate who you are and what you stand for—you have the chance to do extraordinary things by building on your passions and strengths. As you answer the question, "Who are you?" it will also empower you to accomplish extraordinary things.

Understand that part of self-awareness is learning to recognize behavior clues that alert you when you need more stimulation and challenge or when you need to pace yourself, take a break, or mix up a routine. You need to know what drives you on your success journey, and what you're made of. That's what we'll explore next.

WE HAVE TREMENDOUS POWER OVER RESCRIPTING OUR LIVES

CHAPTER THREE

WHAT ARE YOU MADE OF?

"The unexamined life is not worth living."

— Socrates

YOU MIGHT recall a show that was very popular in the 1970s called *The Six Million Dollar Man*, which starred Lee Majors. His character, Steve Austin, suffered a terrible accident—but then a government experiment turned him into a sort of robot-human hybrid with superhuman abilities. He was rebuilt better than he was before.

What if *you* could rebuild yourself? If you had a choice of attributes and talents laid out on a table in front of you and you could transform yourself with them, which ones would you choose?

Know that to a large degree, you *can* make yourself better. In fact, I believe that if you work at it, you can and should try to improve yourself each and every day. I'm not talking about plastic surgery or pretending to be someone you're not—I'm talking about something far different; that is, looking for and drawing out the special qualities that are *already* inside you. To borrow a term that Newt Gingrich once used to apply to the economy, it's all about "insourcing" your talents for a better life.

The Art of Insourcing:
Getting a "Sense" of What You're Good At

We need our senses to help us survive. However, they can also serve to guide us by helping us develop greater self-awareness. We can discover some of our talents and interests by literally following our nose . . . or any of our five-plus senses (I say "plus" because many people refer to a sixth unofficial sense, which may be a gut feeling, or it may be their conscience):

1. Some people get the greatest satisfaction from using their sense of **touch**. In fact, many of the most gifted people in the world make their living and leave their legacy with their hands: think about surgeons, carpenters, sculptors, and dentists.

2. Individuals with a strong sense
   of **vision** enjoy not just looking
   at things but "seeing" them;
   that is, really taking the time to
   observe the world with their eyes.
   Bird-watchers, scientists, graphic
   designers, astronomers, and pilots
   all are successful at their work or
   hobby through the use of their keen
   eyesight.

3. As for the sense of **smell,** humans
   don't come anywhere near the
   olfactory ability of our four-legged
   best friends, yet some people do lead
   life "by the nose." They really do stop
   and smell the roses—and maybe they
   also grow, maintain, or sell them.
   They judge wines by their bouquet;
   they research and develop scents for
   perfumes, candles, and air fresheners;
   they work at food corporations
   and restaurants, and at spas as
   aromatherapists; and they can detect
   signs of danger such as smoke, gas
   leakage, mold, or fermentation long
   before others are aware of these odors.

4. **Hearing** is something we often take for granted . . . until we start to lose it, that is. It's true that people who lack one sense have more developed remaining senses: Some of our most talented musical artists, such as Stevie Wonder, Ray Charles, and Andrea Bocelli, have been blind or visually impaired for all or most of their lives. (Sound engineers, audiologists, orchestra conductors, and speech therapists are all possible careers for the aurally inclined.)

5. Many people would probably love to make a career out of their sense of **taste**! If that's you, know that food corporations at many levels do need research-and-development people who are professional tasters. And chefs and food critics seem to have pretty good gigs going as well.

By recognizing that clues to self-knowledge are all around us, we can let our senses guide us to our passions. They may lie right in front of our eyes (or ears or hands . . .).

Rescripting Your Life

My friend and mentor Stephen Covey and I strongly agree that we should all live out of our imagination, not our history. Even though this book is called *Who Are You?*, I want to emphasize that it's not just about who you were or who you are now, it's also about who you envision yourself to be in the future. That's the message I hope stays with you throughout this self-discovery process— and throughout your life as well. You can hold a vision of the possibility of a better life for you and yours, and you can take responsibility and exercise the faith and power you have within you to create that better life.

We have tremendous power over rescripting our lives. I go into more detail about this in some of my other books, but to sum it up, the "Three C's" in this process are confidence, competence, and capability.

The Three C's are all you need, plus some time—after all, it's been said that "humor is tragedy plus time." It's true that when we're very close to an unfortunate situation, such as a failure or loss, there's nothing funny about it. But with time, and a positive attitude that accepts that we all have our ups and downs and growing pains, we may be able to find some humor—or at least some wisdom—in our experience.

The truth is that unless we're extremely fortunate, our history is probably dotted with our share of struggles. They may have been emotional, financial, or familial; we may have lacked education, wealth, a safe environment, guidance and support, fairness, or even basic necessities. We all have hurts, and it's easy to place blame on others and play the victim. The problem with that role is that it's so limiting—we see ourselves as the product of a negative experience or environment with little control over our present and future. The term *self-fulfilling prophecy* remains a popular expression for good reason: There's some truth to becoming what we're labeled—but only if we're content to hang on to those labels or are afraid to challenge them and create new images of ourselves.

We base our feelings about a situation or a relationship on our own singular perspective—well, who says that perspective is correct or even objective? We all come to every situation with preconceptions, biases, and an emotional state of being; consequently, our interpretation of events may be driven by our self-esteem—or by values taught to us by family members, religious doctrine, or even the media. These can all cloud our perception of reality. The result is that we often feel

hurt, angry, guilty, or unnecessarily disappointed because we simply misinterpreted someone else's comment, expression, or expectation.

Each and every one of us has emotional baggage, but that doesn't mean we have to carry it around with us wherever we go. We all need to let go of the past, or it will trip us up in the present and future. It's vital that we clean house from time to time so that we're free to move forward.

Toss, Keep, and Repair

In order to "clean house," I've adopted the sorting system some professional organizers use when helping pack rats clear their space: *toss* (or donate), *keep,* and *repair.* You can use this technique as you mentally take stock of your personal and professional victories and losses, relationships that didn't work out, and skills you have or want to improve upon. Keep it as simple as possible, and keep sorting. By the end of the process, you should know what you like about yourself (which you'll keep intact), what you need to work on (or new skills and attitudes to develop), and what goals are worthy of your time and energy for the short- and long-term. Leave the rest in the past where it belongs.

This may not be the easiest exercise because it can be hard to part with baggage you've had for so long—it can almost feel as if it's a part of you. But there *is* a time to give yourself permission to live in the present and plan for the future without "tainted glasses." It may mean that you let go of your dream of playing professional sports (or that your son or daughter will). It may mean that you come to terms with the fact that you'll never be able to repair a relationship you damaged. It may mean that you change your annual health goal from losing 20 pounds to just eating better and exercising consistently.

When you sort through your life and take a realistic look at your past and present balance sheet, you're well on your way to making self-awareness work for you. In the next chapter, as we take a look at challenges and opportunities across the human life span, keep that balance sheet in mind and see if there are any adjustments you'd like to make. Each of us is a work in progress, after all.

NO MATTER
WHAT STAGE
OF LIFE
YOU FIND
YOURSELF IN,
AIM TO MAKE IT
THE BEST ONE

CHAPTER FOUR

THE STAGES OF LIFE

"You've got to get to the stage in life where going for it is more important than winning or losing."

— Arthur Ashe

THE PERSON you are transcends past, present, and future categories—that is, your core values, beliefs, disposition, and talents largely remain unchanged over time. Therefore, assessing who you are is a process that looks at all your goals (past, present, and future) to identify those essential aspects.

In my seminars, I talk with participants who are at different stages of their lives yet grappling with common issues. It's noteworthy that as uniquely individual as we all are, collectively we tend to go through the same specific challenges, passages, or crises at certain points in time. Some incredibly astute people have spent much of their lives mapping out these stages so that individuals and society as a whole may benefit by planning and preparing for them. While pioneers such as Sigmund Freud stopped exploring the stages of life at the end of childhood, others (including social psychologist Erik Erikson) took up where they left off and found evidence that we continue to grow and evolve well into adulthood.

I find that this information is especially helpful in telling young people about the "Stages of Life," since they don't really have an understanding of how the process of living works. They need to "get" how it will affect their futures if they don't meet some important milestones early on. In other words, they need to put in work on the front end, or they're going to lose out on the back end of life.

Young people want instant gratification. They live in the present, on a day-to-day basis, so when I present examples of likely future consequences of their actions, it wakes them up. It also gives them an idea of how to visualize their future—not just 5 years from now, but 50 years from now. It's wonderful for them to begin to look at their entire life and begin to frame it based on the direction *they* want to go.

Following is my basic interpretation of the Stages of Life, based on what I've learned through my experience as a social worker and educator, as well as from my interactions with the people I've met over the years:

1. Youth

Age	Stage
1–4	Early childhood
5–13	Elementary school
14–17	High school

2. Young Adulthood

Age	Stage
18–22	Vocational school/college; select career, occupation
23–25	First job
26–30	Gain real-world knowledge; invest in yourself

3. Adulthood

Age	Stage
31–40	Advance career; develop expertise and relationships
41–50	Apply expertise in career and community
51–55	Enjoy lifestyle; mature career
56–65	Legacy established; retirement

4. Older Adulthood

Age	Stage
66–75	Continued contributions
76–84	Elder statesperson
85+	Enjoy life

The First Stage of Life: Youth

Early Childhood (Ages 1–4)

These early years of childhood are the most critical of your life because the gains made at this time are exponential. A lot of your attitudes and habits are cultivated here: You're very impressionable, and your parents or caregivers have a great influence on your outlook on life and your daily activities. So, without realizing it, you're gaining an understanding of trust by discovering who can be counted on to meet your needs. The world revolves around you (why shouldn't it?), yet you're also learning to interact with others. It's also a time when (hopefully) you've figured out how to soothe yourself in times of distress.

Much of the human personality is formed by age five; even twins who share the same genetics and environment show distinct personalities. Kids are

very resilient, but damage done during this period can have lifelong effects. So what happens if you don't learn to attach to, and feel secure with, others during this time? Well, it can have a tremendous impact on how you approach relationships, along with your ability to cope throughout life.

It's natural for children to want to play and to explore the world. Everything's new and amazing to a young child, and it's supposed to be that way. Whether you play with other kids or by yourself with toys, you're developing skills and interests during this period that will set the stage for success. If you can't derive pleasure from activities, you're actually considered dysfunctional. If you find very few activities gratifying, you won't develop a repertoire of skills and the problem-solving abilities of your peers. The result? You'll lack a sense of success and may get bored or overly emotional. When challenged, you'll often give up in frustration and avoid involvement altogether.[1]

Childhood is a time of learning to process both thoughts and feelings, a time when we gain the ability to think. We learn by a combination of trial and error, by someone else's example, and by repeating or practicing a new skill over and over. This learning and processing will continue to develop throughout our lives, but as we get older it takes conscious effort.

WHO ARE YOU?

Elementary School (Ages 5–13)

According to Sarah Thompson, vice president of education at the Nashville Chamber of Commerce, "Teachers say they can tell by the fourth grade who the 35 percent of kids are who are going to drop out of school."[2]

Isn't that amazing? Kids in fourth grade are only nine or ten years old! The message here is that adults can truly help children start on the right foot in life by showing interest in what they're doing in school, who their friends are, and what they enjoy the most. The value of children's confidence cannot be overstated.

Kids develop confidence by mastering new skills. Think about that, because that concept really sticks throughout our lives. When we have a task that's challenging but not overwhelming and we succeed at it, it makes us feel good about ourselves. In other words, something we did had an effect, and we're better for it.

High School (Ages 14–17)

What happens if you don't finish high school? I tell young people that if this happens to them, then their life is predestined. I can predict, with some degree of certainty, what type of job and lifestyle they'll have and the struggles they'll face. Do I have a special gift of clairvoyance that allows me to gaze into the future? No—I've just seen what happens to dropouts too many times to count.

You've probably heard the proverb "Failing to plan is planning to fail," and it's true—I see the sad consequences of that again and again. Without at least a high school diploma, a young person is at a serious disadvantage.

Here are just a few statistics to illustrate my point:

- Dropouts are about three times as likely to be welfare recipients compared to those who graduate.[3]

- Men and women aged 25–34 who dropped out of high school earned 27 and 30 percent less, respectively, than their peers who had a diploma or GED (general equivalency diploma).[4]

- The unemployment rate for high school dropouts was 30.8 percent in October 2003.[5]

- On average, graduating from high school rather than dropping out means $270,000 more in earnings over a lifetime. Graduation also opens the door to further education and opportunity: College graduates in turn earn about $1 million more than high school graduates.[6]

- More than 80 percent of the 23 million jobs that will be created over the next ten years will require at least some postsecondary education.[7]

We all must have a starting point, or a foundation for development. Think of it as building a house: If the foundation isn't solid, the structure that gets built on top may be shaky as well. Likewise, a solid foundation in your education can support each subsequent level of learning and achievement. If you're in high school and thinking about dropping out, please don't. And if you never finished high school, know that getting your GED will change your life—not only in terms of the opportunities that will open up to you, but also in the way your self-confidence will blossom.

The Second Stage of Life: Young Adulthood

Vocational School/College; Select Career, Occupation (Ages 18–22)

During this stage you may really think that you know what you want to do in life. That's no surprise, and you're in good company because so much focus in our nation today is to "be something." Yet as I've already expressed, my concern is that students are rarely encouraged to know who they *are* as a basis for who they want to *become*.

Whether from family, peers, or the media, young people hear messages all the time about what kind of vocation they should pursue. Now some careers may sound glamorous or lucrative from an outsider's perspective, but they may not be that way at all in reality (or only for a select few). I felt that I had to write *Move Without the Ball*, a book about planning for a life outside sports, because the majority of young people I'd met told me that they wanted—and planned—to play professional ball. Can you blame them for desiring the kind of life they see professional athletes, film and TV stars, or rappers leading? Such individuals always seem happy, they're surrounded by beautiful people, and they can buy anything they want. Of course, much of this may be an illusion—or it's a quick rise to fame with a quick fall, too—but that doesn't get a lot of attention, so we forget that it happens all too often.

If you do choose a field of study or career for what I'd call "the wrong reasons" (money, fame, or popularity), I'll save you some time: It's not going to work out. It won't sustain your interest. It won't make you feel like a whole person. Instead, you need to select a career that makes you feel good about yourself and what you're contributing. And you need to feel fully engaged to endure the highs and lows of any profession. No job is a sure thing anymore—as scary as this might sound, it's also very freeing. You don't need to go into something you're not passionate about just so that you can get a high-paying job. In a couple years, those jobs might not be so high paying or in demand anymore.

College and Commencement

Today's college students have more options—and more challenges—than ever before. Competition is tougher; technology and subject matter change rapidly; and the marketplace they're preparing for is global. Demands, requirements, and rules in nearly every profession are in flux, as is access to

resources. We live in a performance-based culture, which means that it matters less and less where you're from, what your race or gender is, or even what college or university you attended—what matters today is how you're able to interact and produce results.

As fun as the college years can be, this is also a serious period when you're laying the groundwork for the type and level of knowledge and skills you'll need to meet the challenges of our information age. In addition, it's a time to work on getting along with (and even living with) people who may be very different from you.

Newfound independence is exciting, but it's not always easy. You may struggle with balancing your time between studying, working, sleeping, and socializing. You may not realize how important it is to eat well and take good care of your body without a parent telling you what to do or making sure that you do it. You'll likely test your boundaries and be tested in many ways: Many college students are faced with peer pressure, low self-esteem, a lack of vision, and poor academic performance.[8] And non-academic concerns for college students, such as alcohol abuse and financial debt, continue to be widespread.

You need to draw from your inner strengths and discipline yourself so that you can cope with the pressures, challenges, and changes of this stage of life—and focusing on what you want to do when you're *out* of college will help you do so.

As an aside, here's what happens when college students, even those we think of as academic achievers, don't have a sense of who they are. According to a report by the University of Tennessee, most first-time, full-time freshmen who start at four-year colleges don't complete a degree within six years, while others spend years switching majors trying to figure out what they really want to do with their lives. More than a few college graduates enter the job market, discover little demand for their skills, and settle for underemployment. Even many established, college-educated professionals are unhappy with the career choices they've made and yearn to do something more rewarding.[9]

First Job (Ages 23–25)

Not too long ago, young people with a college degree could be fairly assured that success was within their grasp. College graduates had an unwritten grace period at their entry-level jobs during which they could learn the competencies and "soft skills" of their position and of the

workplace in general. Career paths were fairly straightforward—it was uncommon to work for more than three companies during a lifetime, and only a small percentage of the workforce changed careers completely.

Today, too many students still graduate from college without the skills and attitudes it takes to get and hold a job. Employers are spending tens of millions of dollars a year on *remediation,* that is, trying to correct deficiencies in skills such as reading and writing. Companies are struggling to instill such basic attitudes as a strong work ethic and a sense of responsibility in many of their employees, and managers are scrambling to find enough competent candidates to fill available jobs.[10] With the pace of business in nearly every field, there's now no "downtime" or grace period during which new graduates can adapt to the work environment.

Adjusting for inflation, salaries are getting lower today as big companies outsource their labor and tighten their budgets. Competition is more intense, technology has decreased the need for manual labor, and global communication and trade have eliminated many jobs that people once counted on. This is nothing new, really: The Industrial Revolution made many agrarian jobs irrelevant, and now the "Information Revolution" has arrived full force, with the Internet's exchange of ideas and global trade at an unprecedented level.

Today, the unimaginable is reality: Who would have thought that one day "American" cars would be made in Mexico and "Japanese" cars would be made in the U.S.? Or that my 81-year-old neighbor and friend would be using a computer—let alone the Internet—and speaking to a customer-service representative based in India but who is employed by a U.S. computer manufacturer? Outsourcing and immigration aren't going to go away, no matter how much some people want them to. The truth is that these things eventually boost our economy because they make us innovative by keeping us competitive and growing.

We can no longer expect traditional office or factory jobs that pay great salaries and provide wonderful benefits to be there for us, especially for new grads trying to get their feet wet; nine-to-five positions are also getting scarcer. On the positive side, we have the freedom and the ability to create the job we want in the environment we want to work in with the hours we want to work. Young people now even dictate whether they're going to wear business, business-casual, or just plain casual attire for work. The dot-com boom may be over, but

the paradigm shift in the way we think of work has just begun. This is a good thing: Even entry-level workers in their early 20s are considering *whole*-life quality, not just work-life quality.

Young people at this stage are also developing more serious relationships. However, times have changed from my generation (and certainly from my parents') in that we no longer expect people to marry before they're 25. The social dynamics have changed, partly due to affluence, partly due to a longer life span—some call this "extended childhood." Kids may even "boomerang" after college and come back to live with their parents.

If you're in this age range, you might not feel like an adult (translation: *responsible*) for a few years, even though you've started your first job. It is a big step, though, and an important time to learn how to live on your own in the real world—to budget your paycheck so that you'll have enough for rent, to pay back college loans, and to save and invest. It's never too early to start planning for the future and building a good credit history. This is a time when people risk hurting themselves on the back end because of a combination of not knowing how to manage their money . . . yet knowingly going for instant gratification.

Gain Real-World Knowledge; Invest in Yourself (Ages 26–30)

This is a time when you're still discovering your strengths and interests—while learning to focus on them, too. At this stage, you can really blossom in your job and in building relationships with others. It's a time to challenge yourself to your fullest by paying attention to how you work best, how well you listen to others, and how you handle stress. There's a lot of drive to achieve at this stage, and if this energy is focused in the right direction—that is, toward your passions and goals—it will serve you well for years to come. However, this is also where you might feel yourself stagnating by holding on to a job you're overqualified for or that you simply don't love. And if you married right out of high school or college, your relationship may take a turn for the worse if you and your partner no longer share the same vision for the future. The longer you stay in these "holding patterns," the harder it will be to break out of them.

With Generation X, we saw the beginning of what some called a "Quarter Crisis": People around the quarter-of-a-century mark who weren't feeling connected to their work, their friends, or their

communities started taking risks. They went back to school to change careers; they quit their jobs to travel abroad; or they packed up their belongings and moved to another city that seemed more exciting or had better job opportunities.

At this stage of life, you have the freedom to take such risks, especially if you have some savings. Here you typically don't have the family responsibilities (such as young children or elderly parents to care for) or strong community roots that people of past generations shared during their mid-through late-20s. You may be anxious about getting stuck in a literal or figurative place that you'll be unhappy with down the line, so this is the time to check out your options—while you still can.

The great thing about the discovery and growth process we're exploring in this book is that your chances for redirecting your life don't end at age 30, and you don't need a "midlife crisis" excuse later on if you change your life course. Opportunities to reinvent yourself—through discovery, redirection of careers or relationships, relocation, and education—are always available to you. (However, most of us are more mobile and open to change during the earlier stages.)

The Third Stage of Life: Adulthood

Advance Career; Develop Expertise and Relationships (Ages 31–40)

The 30s are a time of great focus. You know yourself better after exploring different types of jobs, environments, and relationships in your 20s. You take yourself more seriously now, and others do, too. In your professional life, you're developing expertise in your field and really growing. You know that you still have options open, and it's a turning point—a time to position yourself for the future and really follow your passion.

You seek more stability and depth in your work and social life. You've built a number of relationships, and now you enjoy spending quality time with a smaller group of friends, rather than the large groups of your youth.

This is a decade when many people make the commitment to buy a home and settle down with a partner and start a family. Your financial responsibilities are growing. And even though you still may not feel like an "adult," people are beginning to call you "sir" or "ma'am," and your twentysomething friends are starting to look to you for advice.

Apply Expertise in Career and Community
(Ages 41–50)

Here you begin to think about how you fit into your community—how are you contributing? You want to see yourself as a leader in your family, at work, and in organizations you're associated with. You contemplate giving back: You may decide to serve on a board, become a mentor, or write articles about your area of expertise to share with others in the field. You're probably tired of doing the same thing over and over all the time.

You're starting to feel older, and you realize that your time is limited. You reevaluate your priorities: If you've been very focused on your career, this is the time to step back and focus on fulfillment in your personal life. One recent development has been the explosion of fortysomething new moms and dads. Whether through reproductive technology or adoption, couples who have postponed a family due to career ambitions and/or because they married later in life still have the option of becoming nurturers.

Enjoy Lifestyle; Mature Career (Ages 51–55)

Reaching this stage is a big milestone for people—after all, if you're going to live to be 100, you've lived half your life. Depending on how things are going for you, you might say that these are your best years, the time when you really begin to live your life. You have a greater understanding and acceptance of yourself, you've earned more power and respect in the workplace, and you feel free to express yourself and use your time the way you want to.

However, these may also be the "Sandwich Years," when you feel a tremendous social and financial pressure to continue providing for your children (even including high school or college graduates who aren't independent yet)—and you feel the pull from aging parents as well. You may also be stepping in to help raise grandchildren if both parents need to work full-time to make ends meet. You're truly caught in the middle, and it's important to remember to take care of *yourself* while you're taking care of others.

The positive side is that you've earned others' trust and respect by being dependable, or they wouldn't be leaning on you. Don't lose control: There may be times you need to exercise your boundaries and be realistic about what you're willing to do—and what you're not.

Legacy Established; Retirement (Ages 56–65)

By now you're pretty settled into your lifestyle—yet you're looking for more quality in your life, in your work or leisure, and in your relationships. You want to make your mark.

Keep in mind that for each stage these are ideal milestones, and not everyone will experience these stages in exactly the same way or in such a positive fashion. For example, you may hope that you'll retire between the ages of 55 and 65. It's a socially accepted pattern: You've "paid your dues" by working for 30 or 40 years, and now you're free to enjoy yourself—to travel, to spend time with grandchildren if you have them, or to get back into an old hobby or explore new ones. But in reality, you may not be so lucky. If you haven't planned for these later years of reduced and fixed income, you may find yourself working during this stage to keep up with the cost of living and unexpected expenses. The Gallup Organization has conducted three surveys on retirement for Zurich-based UBS AG, a financial services company, since 1998. That first year, 36 percent of respondents expected to work past age 62; but in 2004, 57 percent shared that expectation."[11] That's a big difference.

Many Americans have found themselves in the position of working into their anticipated retirement years as health-care costs rise for them and their family members. They may also want or need to contribute to the education or rearing costs of a grandchild, or help elderly parents with their living and health-care expenses.

The concept of a period of retirement really isn't that old anyway—it only evolved during the last century as people began to live long enough to retire. This meant that they could no longer participate productively in work, but back then, "work" involved fairly heavy physical labor, whether it was agriculture- or industry-based. Also, the grand notions people used to entertain about retiring are changing as studies and personal experience show it's not really all it's cracked up to be: While some thrive without work, many individuals need the structure, social benefits, and sense of purpose it brings.

So, on a positive note, if you enjoy working and you're healthy enough to continue, there's now less pressure to quit (in fact, it's a healthy choice if your identity is largely tied to work). You can also take this opportunity to redirect your career instead of retiring. You can explore nontraditional work opportunities, for example. You still have more than 20 percent of your life years left, so why not

fill them with activities that give you a sense of accomplishment, purpose, and joy?

The Fourth Stage of Life: Older Adulthood

Continued Contributions (Ages 66–75)

Here you're looking back at what you've contributed to your family and to society. Your kids are grown, and you may be a grandparent. You're searching for a higher quality of life, seeking more outlets for creativity and more avenues to personal growth. You're more spiritual.

You want to travel and do the things you always said you would—yet you may not have that luxury because there are more expenses and responsibilities than you planned for. You may still be working or helping your kids and grandkids, and your parents might still be alive and now even need more attention from you. It's very important to take time for, and take care of, yourself.

Elder Statesperson (Ages 76–84)

Your disposition really shows in this stage, depending on how positive or negative you are about life: grumpy old men may appear grumpier, while sweet little old ladies appear even sweeter and happier. Seen as wise, you know how life works—you've seen and done it, after all—so you offer advice.

You may be stuck on the history of how life used to be. Perhaps you spend a lot of time talking and thinking about the past, reflecting on your accomplishments and failures, and making some amends as you approach your "twilight" years. You may be more tolerant and mellow, and you might be reaping the benefits of the seeds you sowed earlier in life (good or bad). You could be dependent on your family for care, and you're not as independent as you want to be.

Enjoy Life (Ages 85+)

As advancements in health care and medicine improve, more of us will live into our 80s and beyond—even to 100 years "young." At the turn of the last century, life expectancy in the U.S. was 49 years; in 1996, it rose to just over 76 years. When TV weatherman Willard Scott first started his birthday tribute to centenarians, it was a short list—but as of 1990, there were 37,306 of them according to the U.S. Census Bureau. And based

on current population trends, there could be 850,000 centenarians by the year 2050!

If you're one of the fortunate ones to reach this age group, I hope that you'll involve yourself with people, activities, and things that you love and that reflect your authentic nature. Let this be a time of thoughtful reflection and, above all, celebration of the life you've built.

No matter what stage of life you find yourself in, aim to make it the best one. All your experiences, good and bad, make you the person you are today—they bring insight into your capabilities and values, and they shape your character.

We'll continue to assess and define ourselves in the chapters ahead, with this life overview in mind.

WHATEVER YOUR DREAM IS, WRITE IT DOWN

CHAPTER FIVE

WHAT DO YOU WANT TO BE?

"What could be worse than being born without sight?
Being born with sight and no vision."

— Helen Keller

LIFE certainly is rocky—but it's overcoming that rockiness that makes things interesting!

Rock climbing is becoming an increasingly popular sport for individuals of all ages because it's that sense of achievement, the "high" people get from knowing that the climb will be challenging but the end will be rewarding. There's nothing quite like that feeling of standing on the mountaintop and realizing: *I did it. I made it. I accomplished something real.* Just like life, the climb becomes easier and more manageable if you have a clear vision of what you want to attain in mind.

The Importance of Vision

Vision is so important because it prevents you from stumbling into the quicksand of life's disappointments. You're more likely to interpret rocky events as merely temporary setbacks, and you'll have the determination to keep going.

You'll also gain confidence in yourself and your abilities as you reach different levels toward your pursuit. These are milestones (or checkpoints) in your life, such as your first steps, first day of school, confirmation or bar mitzvah, graduation, first job and college, marriage, divorce/loss of spouse, children, "empty nest," and retirement. As you can tell, not all of these are traditionally thought of as positive events, but it's the way you react to them and how you integrate these experiences into your life that matters.

To be successful, you must also have a detailed vision of what success is to you. For example, what does it feel like—are you content, powerful, happy, relieved, or satisfied? At each level you want to reach, keep a picture in your mind of how you want it to be. Remember that there will be lots of pinnacles and plateaus along the way, so these milestones will be a good opportunity for you to look down to see where you've been or how far you've come, as much

as they are a time to see how far you still have to go . . . or grow.

Writing Your Autobiography in Reverse

Have you ever thought about writing your memoirs? You don't have to be famous to do so—*everyone* has a good story. I enjoy reading biographies because I'm always uplifted by the accomplishments of others. This inspiration can lead me to attempt things I might otherwise not have, or it can even reshape my vision of myself.

As you consider your own abilities and desires in the light of what others with similar interests have accomplished, you can refine your vision and gain new energy for achieving it. But now I'm going to ask you to do something a little unusual: Still think about writing that autobiography, but do so *in reverse*. Visualize yourself in your later years, sitting back comfortably and reminiscing about your amazing life. Really allow yourself to consider the greatest possibilities for yourself in detail. Picture the type of home you're living in and what your surroundings look like. See the people around you—maybe a great-grandchild is sitting on your lap, begging you to tell him again how you found the cure for cancer *and* met the spouse of your dreams. Maybe you're playing golf with the President of the United States, and she's asking for your advice. Perhaps a street is being named in your honor because of all the value you've added to your community. Whatever your dream is, write it down.

So now you know the beginning of your life and how you'll enjoy your later years, or what your legacy will be—you just have to fill in the missing pages of your story. What did you do during the middle years that prepared you for the great things you ultimately achieved? What kind of jobs or education did you seek? What types of connections did you need to make, and how did you make them? What did you do for others that earned their respect? What did you have to change about your life in order to improve it? Did your habits, attitudes, priorities, or relationships change along the way?

If you're having trouble with this concept, take an autobiography of someone you really admire, who also has similar interests as you, and break it down chronologically. (Not all autobiographies are written in a strict chronological format, so this is important.) You'll likely see patterns of success— but you may also see where detours were taken or setbacks occurred, and you'll learn how the person you wish to emulate got back on track.

Work

Work has a very important meaning in our society—and it even defines many of us. At a cocktail party, for example, one of the first things we Americans tend to ask each other is, "What do you do?" This is different from how people in other cultures define themselves: whom they're related to, the village they're from, and how they spend their leisure time are all major components of their identity. In fact, many foreign visitors don't understand our preoccupation with jobs and positions at all.

Most of us in the U.S. spend the majority of our waking hours on the job. If we don't get this right— that is, if we're not doing something we love—then we're compromising ourselves and our lives. After all, employment serves several purposes: It can structure our day; it can be a social, physical, or intellectual outlet; it can give us a sense of value; and, of course, it can provide us with a salary and other benefits.

Keep in mind that even though we're the sum total of what we do, not everything we do is work. We each perform many other activities throughout the day and night—some by choice, others through a sense of responsibility, need, or other outside pressure. We have what occupational therapists call "activities of daily living," or those little routines we do almost automatically (like bathing, dressing, and eating). Then we have our leisure-time activities, such as playing basketball, going to a restaurant with family members, working out, e-mailing friends, watching TV, or reading a book. We usually aren't aware of how we spend our days and all that goes into them until we can't do these simple actions anymore—at which point we become very grateful for the gifts and abilities we do have, and we start to evaluate our priorities in life.

It's been famously said that no one on their deathbed ever lamented, "I wish I would have worked more." Well, if we think of work in the way it's always been constructed, that's true—however, if we think and live "outside the box," we just might want to spend more of our time working, because it also incorporates how we choose to spend our leisure time.

Define Yourself

Career counselors and coaches may recommend that you have a 30-second elevator speech or "commercial" prepared in case you share a ride with someone of importance who expresses even a slight interest in you and what you want to do.

This is the sound bite you can also use for that dreaded job-interview question that always comes up: "Tell me a little about yourself."

In the Western world, where time's such an important commodity for working singles, there's now even a practice called "speed dating," where you can meet 25 potential dates in the time you'd spend getting to know one person. The assumption for both employers and potential dates is that the impression you'll make will happen within less than two minutes. They'll make a decision about you, and rarely can you do or say anything in the following 15 to 30 minutes to change their mind. How can they make these important decisions in that short time frame? Well, it's based on what you say and how you say it, your external appearance, and the appropriateness of your behavior in the situation. They'd defend themselves by saying that time is limited, but I really think it's wrong to make such snap judgments about people.

It's all too easy to be placed in a box by others based on how they perceive you. You're approached with preconceived notions and assumptions—based upon your age, race, gender, clothing, speech, posture, weight, or the type of car you drive. And only if you're lucky will you get the opportunity to give them your 20- to 30-second elevator commercial to confirm or change their opinion.

Your Own "Elevator Speech"

Do you have one of these prepared? If you do, how does it go? Is it all about your career ambitions? Does it include anything about your family, community, or leisure interests? (Of course it depends on the situation and whom you're telling your story to—the one you'd use as a "speed dater" is likely very different from a job-interview spiel.)

I want you to take some time to come up with a speech that sums you up to the core—that is, what you love to do, what you care about most, what makes you unique, and what your long-term goals are professionally and personally. If you write it out, don't think too much about making it short enough, just write the first things that come to your mind. Then when you're finished, take out at least half of what you've written down—what remains is the essential you.

Another important thing to consider when defining yourself is to keep it positive. Most of us focus on our negative traits, or we might be too humble to list our best qualities. If you can get someone else to help you with the speech, who respects you for who you are and has known you for some time, that's not a bad idea. If not, try to start your speech by saying, "Some people say I'm . . . " Of course that doesn't mean you have

to believe it about yourself, but it will describe something that others see as part of who you are and what you stand for.

Above all, remember this: *Don't get caught up in labels—live above them.*

Now that we have a better sense of what we want to be when we "grow up," it's time to start the journey and commit to staying the course.

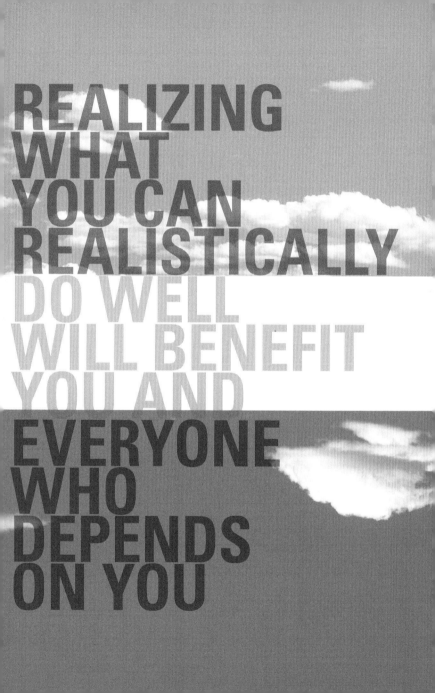

REALIZING WHAT YOU CAN REALISTICALLY DO WELL WILL BENEFIT YOU AND EVERYONE WHO DEPENDS ON YOU

CHAPTER SIX

HOW DO
YOU GET THERE?

"The price of success is hard work, dedication to the job at hand, and the determination that whether we win or lose, we have applied the best of ourselves to the task at hand."

— Vince Lombardi

THERE'S no shortcut to a meaningful life, but there *is* a road map. Just as with any navigation tool, we have to know where we are and where we want to go to determine the most efficient route. If we know where we'd like to end up, then we're more likely to stay on course.

I'd also add that the journey you take is in itself the growth process for finding the true you. You might even decide along the way that a certain path doesn't feel right to you, and you'll learn to trust your instincts as you go along, veering this way or that way to follow your interests or to avoid unforeseen obstacles.

Planning and Persistence

Persistence is crucial to success—in fact, how long we try or how many attempts we make is often the difference between winning or losing in the long run.

You need to keep performing to sustain success. It can be tempting to quit at the earliest sign of trouble, which is what too many people do. You don't want to be like them! Henry Ford got it right when he said, "Obstacles are those frightful things you see when you take your eyes off your goal." How true that is. When you're really focused on success, mountains become molehills, and rivers become puddles to traverse with a little careful planning.

At some of my corporate presentations, I share a favorite poem of inspiration that was written by Dee Groberg and published by my friend Mac Anderson. It's called "The Race," and it tells the story of a young boy competing in a race with peers as hopeful fathers cheer them on. The boy's excitement and eagerness to win and impress his dad trips him up and he falls multiple times, feeling

humiliated and defeated. However, when he sees his father in the crowd, he internalizes the message not to quit, and each time, he gets back up and into the race.

When he approaches his dad apologetically with his head hanging low from defeat, he learns, to his surprise, that by rising each time he fell, he became a winner in his dad's—and the crowd's—eyes. I think that this poem is appropriate for people of all ages because it speaks to the common fear of disappointing others whose opinions we value. Isn't that really why we fear failure? It isn't just about letting ourselves down and not living up to our own expectations; rather, we don't want others to think less of us. We want to see the pride in their eyes as a result of our accomplishments.

With an understanding of this lesson, consider your current pursuit of success. Who is it *really* for? What do you fear the consequences will be if you don't succeed? What can you learn about your own character as you think about how you respond to discouragement or adversity? As the boy in "The Race" did, we too can learn a lot about sustaining our performance and redefining success.

Another story I remind myself of when I'm feeling low is that of Thomas Edison, who is said to have made more than 10,000 attempts before inventing the lightbulb. Of these failed attempts,

79

he said, "They taught something that I didn't know. They taught me what direction to move in."

The Circle Within the Circle:
Creating Value Through Small
but Consistent Successes

Everywhere around us there are things that need fixing or improving. Internationally, there are problems such as war, poverty, and disease—and these same problems can and often do exist within our nation, our state, or even our neighborhood. There are economic, environmental, and humanitarian needs everywhere we turn if we look closely enough. With all the information available to us, we can find out about issues and interests in great detail across the globe. And with so much access to that information, we might think that we have influence and control, even when we don't. We get overconfident when we see some success as a result of our efforts, not realizing that another issue is taking its place or had been there all along. Even the most idealistic thinkers among us know that we can't solve all the world's conflicts.

I'm reminded of Bertolt Brecht's play *The Good Woman of Setzuan*, in which a kind woman's generosity is taken advantage of, and her good intentions lead to more problems. Even in our own lives, our best intentions may be met with failure or undesired results. It's very discouraging, isn't it? Maybe we're students struggling with a particular subject, or we're overweight adults trying to stick to a healthier lifestyle—if we each made a list of everything we want to improve in our lives, let alone in our communities, it would be pretty long. The thought of making real improvements in each area would be overwhelming.

We often hear about how the children of athletes and celebrities struggle with the expectations that others have of them. Even with "nature" (genetics) and "nurture" (growing up with the parent's example and influence) on their side, these kids can still have low self-esteem because they're always being compared to someone else instead of being accepted for who they are. And even if they happen to share some of the same interests and talents as their famous parent, they may not share the same level of ability. Furthermore, the environment the child is competing in may be very different from the one his or her parent succeeded in.

For these young people, I share my "Circle Within the Circle" philosophy: Consider a large project that's made up of many small tasks. It's best to work hard and complete each task, then move on to the next. Picture these tasks as smaller circles within a circle: If you fill in as many smaller circles as you can, then over time you will have filled in the larger circle.

You can't and shouldn't take on all the problems outside your influence—you'll end up losing your focus because it's not possible to do it all. You'll get overwhelmed and discouraged, which is paralyzing. You can be aware of problems in the big picture (or the larger circle), but in reality, you can only control what's in your immediate circle of influence. The Circle Within the Circle has helped me immeasurably in my personal and professional life—I try to do what I can to create successes in smaller circles. Knowing and expanding my circle of influence keeps me engaged in life.

In the '80s, we saw how many people suffered from the "supermom" phenomenon. Instead of a win-win situation, it was "lose-lose" for moms, their families, and their employers. There was such a great desire to "have it all," which translated to the perfect family life and career. Those who accomplished this feat were both admired and

despised, because it wasn't realistic for most people. Some women have since found that they now have a different definition of "having it all": *Quality* time with family is born from *quantity.*

Thanks to the advocacy of many women and responsive corporations (who didn't want to lose their valued employees), there are more flexible work environments for women who still want to be super at work *and* excel at being a mom. The options include flextime, telecommuting, and on-site day care, just to name a few.

Many women also realize that there's nothing wrong with staying home and raising a family, even if most of their peers have careers (often the high cost of child care makes this a practical decision). A number of women choose not to have children because they're very devoted to their work and don't feel that they could meet the needs of a family the way they'd like to. And now it's becoming more common for men to take on the primary caregiver role, while their wives or partners continue with their careers.

There isn't one perfect solution for everyone, but realizing what you can realistically do well will benefit you and everyone who depends on you.

WHO ARE YOU?

Think Globally; Act Locally

If you find yourself stretched in a million directions and going off course, find someone you trust to reel you back in if you can't do it on your own. Remember that bumper sticker that used to be so common: "Think globally; act locally"? That was the right idea. If you're motivated to do something about an issue, you don't have to fly to another continent to make a difference—you'll probably be most effective in the location you're familiar with, in the culture you know, and the language you're fluent in.

Your circle of influence does extend to the community you live in: You can elect your representatives, drive responsibly, recycle, and/or report suspicious activity—all of these things are within your domain and don't require much work. If you feel strongly about something and want to do more, there's always something more that can be done. But just keep yourself focused, and make what you want to do doable and what you want to change changeable.

I hope that you're feeling more confident now about your vision for yourself and how to live it. All that's left to do is keep up your momentum along the journey and keep obstacles out of your path . . . which we'll cover in the next chapter.

WHEN YOU'RE TRULY FOCUSED AND ENGAGED, YOU BECOME THE MASTER OF YOUR DESTINY

CHAPTER SEVEN

CREATE YOUR OWN MOMENTUM

"Imagination is more important than knowledge."

— Albert Einstein

WE'RE ALL BORN creative creatures. Our first artistic expressions may take the form of banging on pots and pans, drawing crayon murals on the wall, or collecting an arrangement of dandelions for a family member or friend. Yet it isn't long before others set limits on our creativity: The wall is *not* a canvas; pots and pans are for cooking, not music; and dandelions don't exactly look stunning in a vase. We may be offered alternative ways to continue to express ourselves, but the impact of limits has already begun to sink in. We no longer have full freedom to express our creative tendencies—they must now become *socially appropriate*. We're told to draw on paper, to bang only on piano keys (and lightly), pick only certain kinds of flowers (and definitely not from the neighbors' yards), and the list goes on.

Unfortunately, it doesn't stop there: In the U.S., creative arts aren't highly valued at all. After all, art and music-education programs are generally the first ones cut from school budgets. And young people are often discouraged from pursuing a serious career in the arts because they tend to be low-paying professions. Yet creativity is one of the most vital parts of ourselves, and we should never completely lose it.

There are many books and seminars available to help you get in touch with your creative side, so I won't go into too much detail about techniques here. There are also puzzles, games, and exercises that stimulate the right brain; and with the explosion of the Internet, it's now easier than ever to be creative. No matter what your interests are, there are so many ideas out there, and they'll inspire you to come up with some of your own. Maybe you'll discover a new way to display your products, an innovative marketing tool, an online course about a subject that excites you, a different career, a desire to be an "armchair traveler" to distant lands, or even a creative name for a new pet. Whatever intrigues you is right at your fingertips.

Drive Your Creativity

Keep in mind that if you think of creativity not only in terms of self-expression, but also as a means to find solutions, it's easy to see how it can be applied to any field: It can exist in business, science, engineering, construction, and manufacturing. In other words, there are always ways to do things more effectively or aesthetically.

One of the most practical approaches to driving your creativity is to consider various scenarios and how you could solve a problem given different tools or resources. Situations, even in business, are more flexible and fluid in reality than most people think—that's why there's been such an explosion in the consulting industry over the last couple of decades. Sometimes it just takes an outsider with a fresh perspective to see how a business can run more efficiently.

One of the things my company does is work with organizations to achieve success by focusing on their strengths, just as I try to do with individuals. It isn't just a matter of cutting personnel and making the remaining employees work even harder—it's about creative solutions, maximizing potential, and not falling into the same patterns that will only lead to the same results. In a competitive global economy, always doing the same thing won't get you very far in the long run. That's why the Nine Steps to Success is so important: The process is a tool to promote innovation and growth through incorporating new ideas and information as they become available.

Energy in Focus:
Energy + Alignment + Time =
Maximum Potential

Energy is a major force in our lives—literally. From the cellular level on up, we're a collection of electrochemical reactions. In physics, energy is the capacity for doing work and overcoming resistance. It's not something we can really witness, although we can certainly see the effects of it—but it's something we definitely feel and sense. We often think of energy as a precious resource and wish we had an unlimited supply. Well, instead of looking for outside sources—such as food, vitamin supplements, or caffeine—we can energize ourselves from within.

Part of learning to understand who you are lies in gaining an awareness of what gives you energy, both positive and negative—be it people, situations, or things. The challenge is in turning negative energy into positive energy to keep up your

momentum. When you generate positive energy—and you're able to align it with what you enjoy doing and what has positive consequences—then over time you'll have an equation for maximum performance that builds upon itself.

Think about how your energy can change in just an instant: You get some bad news. Someone says something rude to you or to someone you care about. A deadline has been changed and it throws off your plans. You're reminded of a sad situation. Your expectations aren't met, even if it's something small like a bad cup of coffee.

By the same token, your mood can change for the better in an instant: You receive a welcome phone call or an unexpected compliment. You find a great parking space, or you catch the bus just as it's about to pull away. Your favorite song comes on the radio. . . . Keep track of these little perks mentally or in writing, and then use this list as a personal reference guide for a quick pick-me-up to counter the things that deflate you. When you refer to your list, let it also be a reminder that these negative moods are fleeting, which may give you some needed perspective before you let things get to you.

You can address "energy drainers" by taking quick mental and physical breaks, using visualization or deep breathing, setting short-term goals to spur you on, mixing up your work tasks, getting up and stretching to get your blood pumping, and changing your perspective by getting some fresh air. You can also try to re-create positive feelings by reflecting on positive past events, and psych yourself up for future events.

But in the here-and-now, how should you react when confronted with negative energy? That's a question most of us have to answer every day. After all, there will always be little things that can bring us down if we allow them to. We haven't invested and believed in ourselves and worked toward our goals all these years to cower or cave in, so why would we want to be so quick to give up our power? Yet with just a slip of the tongue, we can react or overreact in a way that we may regret.

Using Self-Control to Combat Negative Energy

We've talked about self-understanding, self-actualization, self-reliance, and self-acceptance in this book—and another critical component for your lifelong success is *self-control*. You can learn to handle people and situations gracefully, even if they stir strong emotions within you, by setting an example of grace and dignity.

As you become more capable of forgiving your own faults and foibles, you'll be more adept at pardoning others for their baggage and behavior. You'll realize that they have their own slew of programs, labels, and battles to fight, and in their minds, they're doing the best they can with what they have. More often than not, the people who direct negative energy your way may have limited self-knowledge and therefore aren't even aware of how their words and deeds impact the rest of us.

When confronted with a negative person or situation, if you frame it from the perspective that keeps the focus on them, you'll be able to maintain a positive base. You can try to separate the behavior from the individual, understanding that anyone can be susceptible to acting undesirably or losing control under stress. However, even if you're willing to make the effort to think before you act so that you stay in control, you may be wondering what the appropriate way to respond is.

First, ask yourself, *How do I actively make this situation positive? What reaction will I choose?* You may have to tough it out and hold on to the other person's comment for a little bit. Don't absorb the negative energy; don't hold it closely and let it get to you—you'll release it shortly at another time or in another place, just not right now in this situation.

When someone says something to you that you don't like, think of it as though you were handed a dirty diaper: You're caught off guard and not happy about it, but you've got to keep your cool. You wonder, *What are my choices here?* and instead of acting out of anger, you freeze those negative thoughts and actions, say little or nothing at all, get out of the way as quickly as possible, and dispose of it in the nearest receptacle. By dealing with the dirty diaper (that is, negative energy) effectively, you won't let it ruin your otherwise good day. It becomes a non-event and is quickly forgotten, thus holding no shock value or power over you.

When you're able to stop and catch yourself before you escalate a bad situation, you're not only changing the situation and the energy, but you're also improving your ability to exercise judgment and control over your emotions. You have greater self-understanding, and you also understand that your reaction is your choice: You can lash out, or you can turn things around. Sometimes the turnaround isn't evident immediately, but it will happen for you in the long run. *Even if the situation itself doesn't improve, you improve:* You'll be better able to handle yourself and future situations with grace, you'll earn the admiration of others who see your ability to transform negative energy into

positive energy, and you'll be able to activate a part of your brain that looks at the bigger picture (the long term), as well as the true ownership of a problem.

The more you challenge yourself to control impulsive reactions, the more easily you'll be able to create a positive pattern of behavior. You're creating a good habit of thinking and choosing wisely before reacting, and that habit becomes part of your brand of integrity and excellence.

As you practice positive thinking and deflecting negative energy, you'll enjoy greater momentum and discipline to align yourself with your vision and goals. You can then focus your energy on manifesting positive results for yourself and others. You'll have the courage and control to take advantage of opportunities that come your way, both personally and professionally. You'll know that you can handle them; in fact, you look forward to stretching yourself to greatness. When you align outside information, opportunities, and resources—and back them with your internal drive and discipline to succeed—you'll realize your maximum potential over time. You'll make the energy equation work for you.

Distractions, Detours, and Detractors

It's all too easy to retreat back to old ways and patterns, especially negative ones, when you experience what you believe to be failure. Even the most confident among us have periods of low self-esteem and insecurity, so you have to make a conscious, concerted effort to overshadow those feelings with a sense of mastery and success. Don't turn back! Think about the positive aspects of your life and all the positive ways you're going to contribute. Speak to yourself in terms of certainty: *I will succeed,* not *If I succeed.*

Now please understand that when success is individual rather than collective, it can make for very awkward situations. One of the unfortunate realities of achievement is that it can make other people uncomfortable. They may feel inadequate about themselves and act jealous or resentful toward you, and they may try to break your spirit. In my many years of playing basketball (as well as other sports), it was instilled in us as athletes to break the other team's spirit. Once we did, they'd lose their competitive attitude, before finally giving up their hope and confidence as well.

We've talked about labels and how we can accept or reject them—well, keep in mind that labels are yet another way to dampen and damage your spirits. People will test you with them to see how strong you really are, and some of you will be tested every day. For example, if you're a recovering substance abuser, you may have difficulty being around people you know who are still using because there's pressure from these "friends" to fall off the wagon and be like them again. Instead of offering support to you as you try to better yourself, they'll try to keep you in the box by telling you that you'll always be a drunk or an addict.

Beware of those people who try to break your spirit, and stay as far away from them as possible. If you don't, they'll become a threat to you just as they feel you're a threat to them. They may question your decisions or say negative things to undermine your achievements, start rumors to make you look bad, exclude you from social circles and activities, or try to stand in the way of your efforts to prevent you from succeeding. They won't feel satisfied until you're back at their level: defeated.

Sometimes success gives you an opportunity to reevaluate whom you associate with. You want to be around people who are your cheerleaders, not your detractors. You deserve mutual respect in all aspects of your life—so if you find that you have a relationship with another person that always makes you feel bad about yourself, and he or she doesn't appreciate or accept any of your attempts to preserve respect, then it's time to divest yourself of that relationship.

Your associates are an indicator of your value. Just as people gauge a business by its clients or partners, you increase your value when other people of value admire you and want to connect with you either personally or professionally. It's very difficult to change people's minds about you if they don't care about or respect you—it's an uphill (if not impossible) battle. So instead of trying to prove yourself to others, it's better to focus your energy on increasing your inner value . . . eventually, they'll come around. If they don't, at least you'll create friendships with people who like you for the person you are, champion your successes, and hold your best interests at heart. These are individuals who will help you love yourself even more and take pride in what you do. Everything opens up for you when you receive praise and positive energy—otherwise, negativity just breeds more negativity, and it becomes more difficult to overcome obstacles.

Feeling good about yourself is what will give you the strength to make it through the tough times—and even tougher critics. You'll feel enabled to push through the world's pull as it tries to confine and control you. You need to push as much as you can based on what you were designed to do, which is your heart and soul's work. If people try to chip away at you with labels or hurtful actions, they'll still have trouble reaching your heart. (Remember: We reside in the heart.) Always know that nobody can stop you. If you keep coming back to what you love, it will reenergize you, give you your power, help you grow, and sustain your growth. Consequently, you'll find your own voice, your motivation.

If you're successful for the right reasons and are doing something with passion and purpose, peer pressure becomes less relevant. Your goals are what are most relevant to you now, and you're creating the way to lasting happiness. This reminds me of one of my favorite film moments, where a love-struck Gene Kelly dances with his umbrella during a downpour in *Singin' in the Rain:* It may be the perfect example of how happiness on the inside can create an impenetrable shield to what's going on outside.

Focus: The Way to Victory Over Self

As human beings, we're driven by passion, purpose, and energy. The Nine Steps to Success that I've shared in this book involve evaluating what you love most and what you're best at. It also shows you where you need to concentrate more energy. When you focus on what you're good at and what you love, the distractions and detractors won't have the pull on you that they once did. You have an important mission and won't easily be deterred.

When you develop a deep motivation for your personal and professional pursuits, your priorities will come into focus automatically. You won't even be thinking about procrastinating, taking a detour from your calling, or sabotaging your own success. When you're truly focused and engaged, you become the master of your destiny.

You are truly free.

DISCOVERING WHO YOU ARE IS A LIFELONG PURSUIT

AFTERWORD

"It's never too late
to be what you might have become."

— attributed to George Eliot

THE WAY to ensure success in your life is to keep the process of growth constant. For example, time-management experts recommend that you plan your approach for the next workday before you leave the office every night. Ask yourself key questions, including, "How will I use my next 24 hours? What can I do differently that will bring positive results? What small changes can I make to positively impact my career, my family, my friends, and my community?"

Remember, you're preparing for the marathon, not the sprint.

Make Success a Routine: Keep Going and Growing

Discovering who you are is a lifelong pursuit, and you have the potential to increase your personal growth every day. In fact, one of the very exciting and interesting developments of the past couple decades is the number of individuals at or near retirement age who decide to pursue an altogether different career. The amazing thing is that they're choosing to go after dreams that they'd foregone so many years ago. They build a life in semi-retirement or retirement around their true passion—and they become successful at it!

Although such daring is more common in these times when people are living longer and healthier lives, there were others who came before to prove that "it's never too late to be what you might have become." For instance, Anna Mary Robertson Moses had been a hardworking farm wife all her life—well into her 70s. When the physical labor of that existence became too difficult for her, she redirected her energies toward teaching herself how to paint. At age 76, "Grandma" Moses (as she became known) began to create a new legacy, that of one of America's most famous artists. She painted the subject that she knew and loved best: American farm life. She continued her passion of painting until her death at age 101 in 1961.[12]

I wish you a long and engaged life, where all your gifts and talents are put to their highest use; where every day and at every stage you thoughtfully consider what you're doing and why; where you live above labels and create your own energy and value; and where you have clarity about who you are, what you love, where you want to go, and how to get there. And above all, I wish you success.

ENDNOTES

1. Olson, Laurette, "Psychosocial Frame of Reference." In Kramer, P. and Hinojosa, Jim (editors), *Frames of Reference for Pediatric Occupational Therapy* (Baltimore: Williams & Wilkins, 1993).
(**Note:** For more information about childhood development from various perspectives, *Frames of Reference for Pediatric Occupational Therapy* is an excellent resource.)

2. Education Edge, "Learning a Living." Tennessee Department of Education.

3. "School Dropouts: Education Could Play a Stronger Role in Identifying and Disseminating Promising Prevention Strategies." *A Report to the Honorable Jim Gibbons, House of Representatives.* United States General Accounting Office. February 2002.

4. U.S. Bureau of Labor Statistics, as quoted on http://www.pbs.org/now/society/dropouts.html, *NOW with Bill Moyers.* Referenced on http://nces.ed.gov/pubsearch/pubsinfo.asp?pubid=2002114%20.

5. Bureau of Labor Statistics Press Release, April 27, 2004. http://www.bls.gov/news.release/hsgec.nr0.htm.

6. Bureau of Labor Statistics. U.S. Census Bureau, 2003, as quoted in "Kerry Plan for 1 Million More Americans to Graduate High School." May 4, 2004, U.S. Newswire.

7. "Putting Students First: An Analysis of the Potential for Cost Savings and Increased Aid to Students through Greater Participation in the Direct Loan Program." Center

for American Progress. April 29, 2004. http://www.americanprogress.org/site/pp.asp?c=biJRJ8OVF&b=52298.

8. CNN; U.S. Department of Education.

9. Education Edge, "Learning a Living." Tennessee Department of Education.

10. Ibid.

11. Ruffenach, G. "Growing Numbers of Americans Push Back Retirement Dates," *The Wall Street Journal,* October 20, 2004.

12. *The Columbia Electronic Encyclopedia,* 6th ed., 2004, Columbia University Press.

ACKNOWLEDGMENTS

Searching for who you are is a never-ending journey. There's a saying that no one makes it alone. John Donne said, "No man is an island, entire of itself," I'd like to name a few people who have made this project possible:

I want to thank my agent, Jan Miller, who is number one in anybody's book.

I want to thank Louise Hay, Reid Tracy, Jill Kramer, and Danny Levin of Hay House for their leadership.

I want to thank Shashona Chau for her outstanding contributions as Project Director for this book.

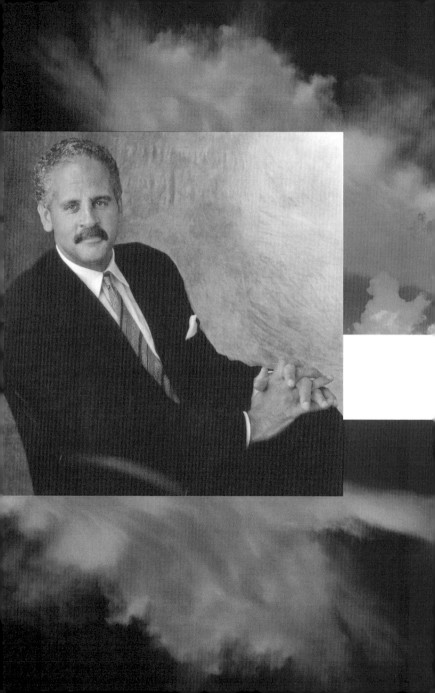

ABOUT THE AUTHOR

Stedman Graham is the author of nine books, two of which (*You Can Make It Happen* and *Teens Can Make It Happen*) are *New York Times* bestsellers. He is chairman and CEO of S. Graham & Associates, a management and marketing consulting firm specializing in both the education and corporate industries; and he speaks internationally to corporations, organizations, and nonprofits. Stedman also serves on numerous boards and is the founder of The Leadership Institute of Chicago and Athletes Against Drugs.

Website: **www.stedmangraham.com**

We hope you enjoyed this Hay House book.
If you'd like to receive a free catalog featuring additional
Hay House books and products, or if you'd like
information about the Hay Foundation, please contact:

Hay House, Inc.
P.O. Box 5100
Carlsbad, CA 92018-5100

(760) 431-7695 or (800) 654-5126
(760) 431-6948 (fax) or (800) 650-5115 (fax)
www.hayhouse.com

Published and distributed in Australia by:
Hay House Australia Pty. Ltd. • 18/36 Ralph St.
Alexandria NSW 2015 • *Phone:* 612-9669-4299
Fax: 612-9669-4144 • www.hayhouse.com.au

Published and distributed in the United Kingdom by:
Hay House UK, Ltd. • Unit 62, Canalot Studios
222 Kensal Rd., London W10 5BN • *Phone:* 44-20-8962-1230
Fax: 44-20-8962-1239 • www.hayhouse.co.uk

Published and distributed in the Republic of South Africa by:
Hay House SA (Pty), Ltd., P.O. Box 990, Witkoppen 2068
Phone/Fax: 27-11-706-6612 • orders@psdprom.co.za

Distributed in Canada by:
Raincoast • 9050 Shaughnessy St., Vancouver, B.C. V6P
6E5 • *Phone:* (604) 323-7100 • *Fax:* (604) 323-2600

Tune in to **www.hayhouseradio.com™** for the best in
inspirational talk radio featuring top Hay House authors!
And, sign up via the Hay House USA Website to receive the
Hay House online newsletter and stay informed about what's
going on with your favorite authors. You'll receive bimonthly
announcements about: Discounts and Offers, Special Events,
Product Highlights, Free Excerpts, Giveaways, and more!
www.hayhouse.com